THE UNAUTHORIZED CARDI B GUIDE TO SUCCESS, LOVE & INTIMACY

THE UNAUTHORIZED CARDI B GUIDE TO SUCCESS, LOVE & INTIMACY

An Exquisite Collection of Her Finest Quotes

A Parody by Bronx Publishing

First published 2021
Reprinted 2022

ISBN: 9798519805254

Cover artwork by Rob Allen
Typesetting and layout support by Karl Hunt

“Imma be the way I am ’til I die, and if YOU don’t like it, die first BITCH.”

Dedicated to everyone who sees the wisdom under Cardi’s snarl.

CONTENTS

INTRODUCTION

A new queen has arrived, and she isn't leaving anytime soon. Cardi B is one in a billion. Maybe one in 7 billion.

Uncompromising and unapologetic, between her record-breaking, award-winning music and authentic artistry, it's no surprise that Cardi B has become one of the fastest rising and most loved rappers of her generation.

A rare hybrid, she is renowned equally for both her music and her personality, but which one dominates? After all, Cardi herself has quipped,

> *"I don't want my personality to overshadow my talent."* (p. 99)

Now in this rare book – a collection of Cardi's most honest thoughts ever recorded on success, love, intimacy and more – you can reflect on what makes this next generation celebrity's personality such a force, and why she's as much a musician & artist as she is a comedian.

Inside you'll find unique new insights, such as Cardi's love for budgeting, distaste for threesomes, and insecurities about whether men really love her for her, or just love the clout. If you're lucky, you'll even be able to apply some of Cardi's wisdom to your own life.

Whatever you take away, keep one thing in mind: Cardi came from the bottom. At age 18 she worked as a cashier at a grocery store and was fired for being late. She worked as a stripper to make ends meat. She's been in 13 fist fights. All this and she still clawed her way up to become the first female solo artist ever to win Best Rap Album of the year at the Grammys, and even interviewed presidential candidates Joe Biden and Bernie Sanders.

As she says in the track 'Best Life', she's a "rose that came from concrete", and we can all aspire to the same growth.

Enjoy this book, laugh, get inspired, share it with friends, and don't forget, as Cardi says on page 43,

"I love you bigger than my ass—and my ass is big."

SUCCESS

“Get yourself together, BITCH.
Learn how to budget, HO.”

"I've been hanging around a lot of people that's wealthy, that is rich, that is FAMOUS. One thing I learned is that no matter how much money you have, no matter how BIG you are, how famous you are, they will still end up stealing your charger and your lighter."

"I always used to think that I was WEIRD. Every guy I dated told me I was weird. In school people always told me I was weird. I soon realized I wasn't weird. Everybody was just BASIC."

until the day I die.”

"The first splurge that I did, I bought, like, an $80,000 watch, but that's because I'm a rapper. I need jewelry."

"This is my WORK ETHIC: I do not want to raise my future kids where I was raised, and I know the only way to do it is working, working, working, working, working."

"I do feel kind of guilty sometimes 'cause, like, I could buy myself a $5,000 dress or a $3,000 dress, and I'm buying these things, but I'm knowing that my cousin need money for the rent. And then I gotta tell myself, 'Stop feeling GUILTY. You worked for this.'"

**“Always have a GOAL.
Always have a second PLAN.”**

"You wanna know how RICH people like me stay rich? By staying on a budget."

"That's why I be so CAREFUL with my money and always try to invest. I see people who have it all and then LOSE it."

"I only FUCK with people who are secure enough to be happy for me and hype me up. I don't want any friends who fall SILENT during my success."

"The faster I make a lot of MONEY, the faster I can have these KIDS I want."

"I just want to tell you college kids that I know sometimes it gets DISCOURAGING, because you see people around your age making money on INSTAGRAM . . . Don't get discouraged, just see it as my WEALTH and my richness is on layaway."

"You don't gotta kiss ASS, but you gotta BE consistent."

"I have a PASSION for music, I love music. But I also have a passion for MONEY and paying my bills."

"I need to make money for my FAMILY and my future family. I'm not a YOLO person."

“What counts the most for WOMEN is having the CONFIDENCE to make your own money.”

"Make MORE than the guys you thought you wanted to be with."

"I'm going to **ENCOURAGE** any type of woman. You don't have to be a woman like me for me to encourage and support you and tell you, 'Yes, **BITCH**, keep on going.'"

"But being a **FEMINIST** is real simple. It's that a woman can do things the same as a man. Anything a man can do, I can do. I can finesse, I can hustle. We have the same **FREEDOM**. I was top of the charts. I'm a woman, and I did that. I do feel **EQUAL** to a man."

"If you WANT it, the more you keep hearing you can't have it, you just GO and GET it."

“Do whatever YOU have to do. People always want to tell you how to do it. No, do it your way. And don’t ask for like, ‘Oh how can you do it?’ Do it. Figure IT out. I figured it out one way or another and I DID it.”

"I cannot turn my LIFE back around. I'm already a public figure, I'm FAMOUS . . . It's like, I might as well keep it going, might as well make the money."

"Am I ever gonna grow THICK skin? No. I just gotta focus on making money. Cause ain't no going back. I'm gonna be famous FOREVER."

"The women that INSPIRE me to be honest are the women that STRUGGLE."

"You better realize your WORTH and stop settling for bare minimum half-ass SHIT."

"It's not that people **WANT** to be like me. But some want to say the things I say, and can't, because they're **AFRAID**. I say it for them."

"A lot of people always QUESTION, 'What else can she do? What else can she do?' And I'm gonna SHOW you."

"I was always SCARED to follow my dreams because if I follow my dreams and I fail, I can't DREAM about it anymore. It's easier to settle for less."

"Music NEVER felt like a job."

"I want a certain type of
RESPECT on my name."

“I’m on my phone 24-7. I see everything. I hear everything. I am the VOICE of the streets.”

"I'm about this **SHMONEY**."

"It's just like, DAMN – I'm competing with MYSELF."

"Imma be the way I am 'til I DIE,

and if you don't like it, die first

BITCH."

LOVE

"Don't rush because you're COLD, BITCH. Get a coat. You don't want to get somebody you don't like . . . you don't need a MAN."

"I could really make a song of HURT, because I've been hurt by a lot of men . . . And I never talk about that because I REFUSE to let people know that I get sad when a man don't ANSWER my calls."

"I love you bigger than my ASS— and my ass is BIG."

“I’d rather have MONEY and be broken-hearted than be BROKE and broken-hearted.”

“I’m an emotional **GANGSTER.**
I CRY once every month.”

"Once a guy has **SEX** with you more than five times, he **LOVES** you."

"Every woman, I think, wants to get MARRIED and wants to have CHILDREN."

DEEPER THOUGHTS ON LOVE

"I have so much ex-boyfriends that did me so FILTHY, and it's like all of a sudden they wanna treat me like they want to be with me again? You wanna treat me like I'm GOLDEN? It's like, I'm still the same girl. I still got the same vagina. I still got the same ASS. I still talk the same. I still cook the same."

"I just be feelin like sometimes I even catch myself telling the guy that I'm dealing with like, 'You don't LOVE me. You just love me cuz I am who I am. The reason why you don't leave me is because I am who I am.' Because I've been doing FUCKING grimy shit to these guys, and they don't leave me. And it's like why are you not leaving me? Because I AM who I am?"

"I feel like people don't even LOVE me anymore for Bacardi Belcalis. People love Cardi B. I feel like sometimes people don't even love me for me. I feel like people just love the CLOUT. People like the fact that like, yeah my girl got money now. My girl is a get money bitch. My BITCH gets in here. My bitch is right there. It just made me feel like, wow am I ever gonna find real love for me? Like is anybody ever gonna LOVE me?"

INTIMACY

“Just DON’T do it. Don’t go BUGGIN out with your VAGINA.”

stomach. And my vagina."

"I'm like a CHICKEN nugget or something. You just wanna put your barbeque SAUCE all up on it."

"If I DRINK, it's like, my man is gonna be around, and I'm gonna have SEX."

"I was **SAD**. Oh, my gosh, I'm not getting no dick on my birthday. But I wasn't going to get **DICK** on my birthday anyway, because I got my **PERIOD**."

"Ever since I started using GUYS, I feel so POWERFUL."

"No man wants to accept they could be getting USED for money. But it's OK for them to let us KNOW that they use us?"

"What I'm trying to say to GIRLS is don't let these GUYS be in your head."

"I'm NOT the type of person that just have sex with a guy and it's like 'oh I see you when I see you'. I get in my feelings. I get in my FEELINGS."

DEEPER THOUGHTS ON INTIMACY

"I'm not gonna tell a girl 'you could do whatever you want with your **PUSSY**. It's your pussy.' Because at the end of the day, if you fuck five guys from the same block you will get **SLUT** shamed. And it is not gonna feel good. And it's like oh damn! It's not gonna feel good when people slut-shame you. So just don't do it. Don't go **BUGGIN** out with your vagina. Because trust me, words go around, and the world is **SMALL**. The world is so small."

INTERVIEWER: **"You talked about how you date men but you have fun with WOMEN?"**

CARDI: **"Yes because I, you know, I had sex with women, but I never fell in love with a woman. I never had a girl that I wanted to be my girlfriend, to spend the rest of my life with. I'd be falling in LOVE with men, but I do like to have, you know . . . stuff stuff . . . with women. I'm attracted to women, you know.**

INTERVIEWER: **"So you've had SEX with women. Just the two of you? Or only threesomes."**

CARDI: **"No I had a threesome a couple of times. But when I do it it's just only to SATISFY my dude to get cool points with my dude. But I never really enjoy the intimacy. So I enjoy intimacy with me and a girl. I enjoy intimacy with me and my guy. But when it's the three thing it's just like a SHOW you know? It's just fake like porn. You're just doing it to look good, not because it's like 'cool baby we should have a threesome, I LOVE having threesomes'."**

"People be saying that they love having **THREESOMES**. I don't know how, cuz I just don't really like it. It's like, I can't. **I DON'T** feel good. You can't focus."

STYLE AND BEAUTY

"Whatever hair COLOR I have on my head, that's what decides what type of outfit I'm going to wear, because not everything goes with your hair color. That's why I SWITCH it up."

"Me: unbothered, moisturized, in my lane, well-hydrated, FLOURISHING."

"I feel BEAUTIFUL without makeup on, but when I do put makeup on it just gives me this extra POP."

"I THINK beautiful is looking like you take CARE of yourself."

"You CAN'T tell me that I can't DRESS!"

"SUMMERTIME, this is the time that you FLEX."

"My GUILTY pleasure is smelling my FARTS."

WISDOM

"To me, music is ART and fashion is
art, but fame? Fame isn't art. But the
person you become when you're famous –
your alter EGO – that's art."

"I thought that after giving **BIRTH** to my daughter that six weeks would be enough time for me to recover **MENTALLY** and physically. I also thought that I'd be able to bring her with me on tour. But I think I underestimated this whole **MOMMY** thing."

"If you say that you're HUMBLE, you're not humble. You gotta WAIT until somebody tells YOU that you're humble."

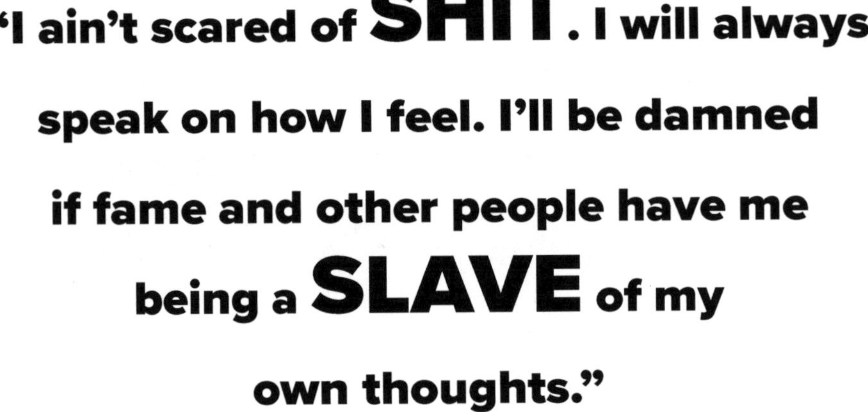

"I ain't scared of **SHIT**. I will always speak on how I feel. I'll be damned if fame and other people have me being a **SLAVE** of my own thoughts."

“Everybody got a **FUCKING** opinion about you. If I change myself, then I’m going to lose myself, and I won’t be who makes me **HAPPY**.”

PRICELESS CARDI GOLD

INTERVIEWER: "How many actual FIST FIGHTS have you gotten in?"

CARDI: 13

"I'm getting my TITS done. I don't give a fuck. Matter of fact, I'm not even going to call it a surgery. I'm just going to say a 'titty renovation' because I got to RENOVATE these shits."

"People be asking me, 'What do you does? Are you a MODEL? Are you, like, a COMEDIAN or something?' Nah, I ain't none of that. I'm a hoe. I'm a STRIPPER HOE. I'm about this shmoney."

"When I talk, I make a lot of MISTAKES. Like, I might say words and the words are not even in the dictionary. But people still like it because you can tell that I'm saying it from the HEART."

"People say, 'Why do YOU always got to say that you used to be a STRIPPER? We get it.' Because y'all don't respect me because of it, and y'all going to RESPECT these strippers from now on. Just because somebody was a stripper don't mean they don't have no BRAIN."

"That soap gave me the YEAST INFECTION of 2017!"

“My mom kicked me OUT a couple of weeks before my 18th birthday. I had a job for about six, seven months at a supermarket, and they FIRED ME for being late.”

"**I WORKED** at this supermarket called Amish Market. Everything is, like, **ORGANIC.**"

"My personality is

HUMONGOUS.

I don't want my personality to

overshadow my TALENT."

“I’m so FREE-SPIRITED. Everyone has a me inside them: that loud girl that just wanna go, ‘AYYYY!’ No matter if you a doctor, a lawyer, a teacher, it comes OUT.”

"People want me to be so full of SHAME that I used to dance. I would NEVER be ashamed of it. I made a lot of money. I had a GOOD time, and it showed me a lot."

"I'm not as OPEN as I used to be. I'm a little bit more filtered, and it kind of SUCKS, but it's the price you pay to get paid."

"My sister's name is Hennessy, so everybody used to be, like, 'BACARDI' to me. Then I shortened it to Cardi B. The 'B' stands for whatever, depending on the day . . . BEAUTIFUL or BULLY."

"It's NOT that people want to be like me. But some want to say the things I say and can't because they're AFRAID. I say it for them."

“It’s not even the female rappers that are CATTY – it’s the fans. They just want that BEEF.”

"I have 100 percent Bronx **PRIDE**, like it's a country. **I AM** the Bronx."

"Bitch I'm a HUMAN just like you.
I like chicken with BBQ sauce just like you.
THE FUCK."

"I'm gonna be FAMOUS forever."

AFTERWORD

"I'm gonna be famous forever".

There you have it: a final statement that captures the confidence, innocence, and vision of our lady, Cardi B.

A woman who continues to redefine what it means to be honest, shame-free and independent, we love her because she makes us feel, and her music makes us move.

Listen to Cardi's music and you notice something in her voice. It collides with your senses like a Mack truck. There's attitude and street piled up behind each lyric, like water behind a damn. She embodies her voice, becomes it. This is what we can learn from her: to become fully what we do, to embody our words and art with all of ourselves.

Under the brash exterior, in Cardi we find a woman who is in tune with something more powerful than the music industry, her gender, or her past. She's a queen. That's how she started, and that's how she'll finish.

THE END

If you enjoyed this book, please take a moment to give it a 5 STAR review on Amazon. Cardi loves you.

Made in the USA
Middletown, DE
02 January 2024